JONATHAN CAPE   LONDON

The Naked

&

The Dressed

20 Years of Versace By Avedon

THIS IS A GLIMPSE
OF THE IMPASSIONED
SHAMELESS
OPULENT
TITILLATING
SEWMANSHIP
OF THAT DAREDEVIL
MAGICIAN OF ART
AND ARTIFICE
WHO WAS
AND WILL ALWAYS BE
GIANNI VERSACE

Remem

brance
Of
Flings
Past

Lust
&
Found

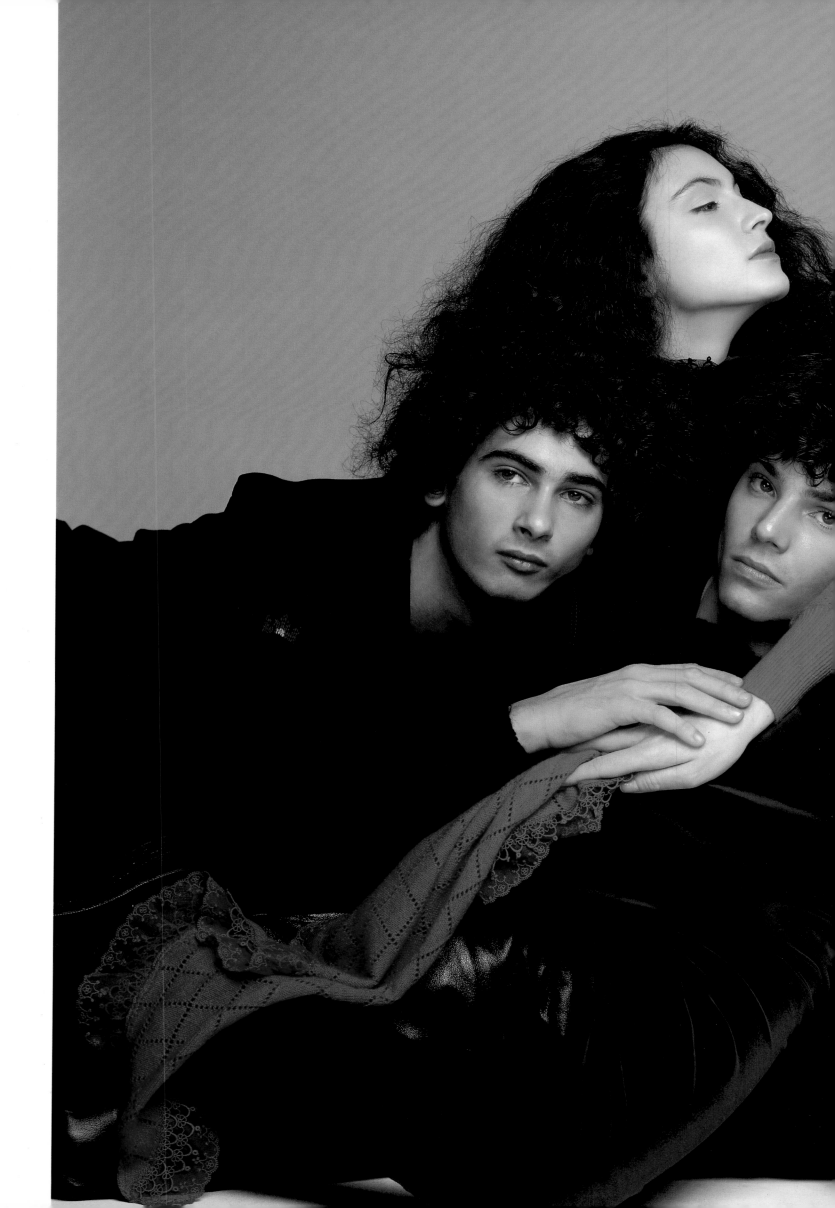

That
Obscure
Object
Of
Desire

Gath-ering

Moss

Gathering Moss

ROCKS AND OTHER HARD PLACES

THE
WAY
OF
ALL
MESH

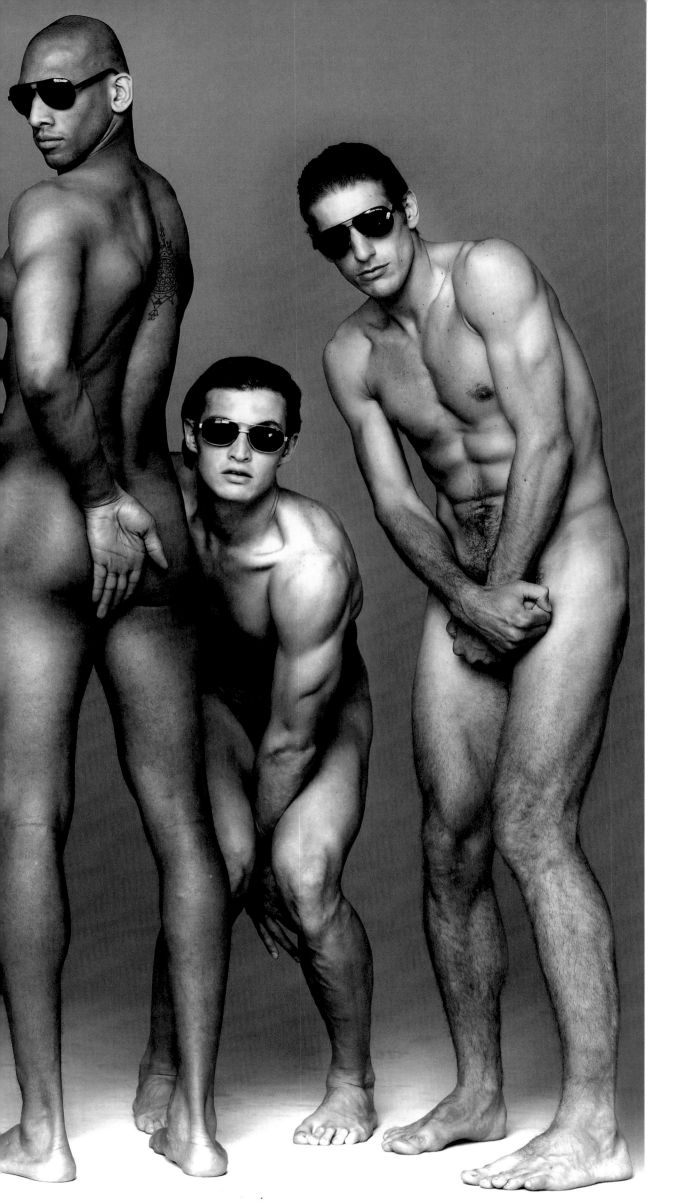

Look Home-ward, Angel

155

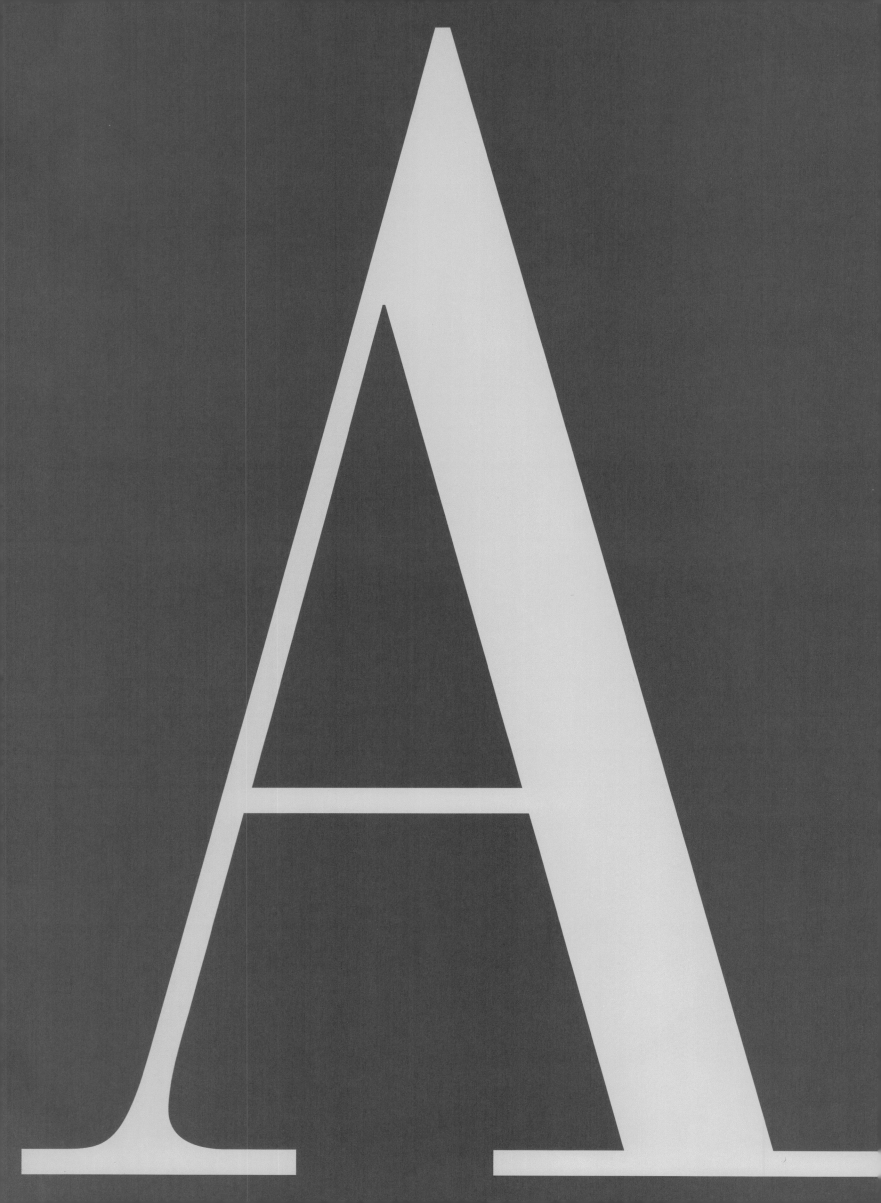

Quick Stitch In Time

Veni, vidi

2. Elton John
Spring/Summer 1997

5.-8. Claudia Schiffer
Fall/Winter 1994/95

Remembrance Of Flings Past

12. Stella Tennant
Spring/Summer 1996, Atelier

14. Karen Elson
Fall/Winter 1997/98

15. The Artist Formerly
Known as Prince
Fall/Winter 1995/96

16. Jon Bon Jovi
Spring/Summer 1997

17. Kylie Bax
*Spring/Summer 1997,
Home*

18. Stephanie Seymour and Marcus Schenkenberg
Fall/Winter 1993/94

19. Cindy Crawford, Hoyt Richards, John Enos and Eric Walters
Spring/Summer 1987

20. Jason Savas and Kelly LeBrock
Fall/Winter 1981/82

22. Maximo and Nadja Auermann
Fall/Winter 1994/95

23. Stella Tennant
Spring/Summer 1997, Home

24. Patricia Arquette
Fall/Winter 1997/98, Atelier

25. Luisa and Jason Savas
Fall/Winter 1981/82

26. Linda Evangelista and Daniel de la Falaise
Spring/Summer 1994

27. Elton John and Kristen McMenamy
Spring/Summer 1995, Atelier

28. Kate Moss
Fall/Winter 1996/97

30. Vladimir
Fall/Winter 1994/95

31. Linda Evangelista
Spring/Summer 1993

32. Chance
Fall/Winter 1994/95

37. Naomi Campbell and
Kristen McMenamy
Spring/Summer 1993

38. Kate Moss and Aya
Spring/Summer 1993

40. Nick Moss, Kate Moss and Aya
Spring/Summer 1993

42. Linda Evangelista and Stephanie Seymour
Spring/Summer 1993

44. Jason Savas, Kelly LeBrock, Rene Russo,
Marcus Abel, Kim Alexis, Alessandro, Anne
Rohart, Iman, Ed Zimlinghaus, Peter Lepore,
Paolo Stoppi and Edourdo Stoppi
Fall/Winter 1981/82

46. Alessandro, Rene Russo and Jason Savas
Fall/Winter 1981/82

48. Jerry Hall and Rosie Vela
Fall/Winter 1982/83

50. Dante, Rene Russo, Kim Alexis and Leo
Fall/Winter 1981/82

52. Danny Arguelles, Jerry Hall and
Quentin Hunt
Fall/Winter 1982/83

54. Joe Dakota and Jerry Hall
Fall/Winter 1982/83

56. Dante, Anne Rohart, Peter Lepore, Kelly
LeBrock, Edourdo Stoppi, Alessandro and
Jason Savas
Fall/Winter 1981/82

58. Beverly Johnson, Joe Dakota, Rosie Vela,
Danny Arguelles, Jackie Adams, Grant Alexander,
Jerry Hall, Quentin Hunt, Tony Hamilton, Gia,
Rick Edwards and Kelly Emberg
Fall/Winter 1982/83

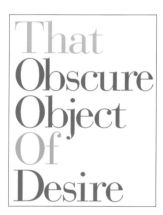

That
Obscure
Object
Of
Desire

63. Elton John
Spring/Summer 1997

64. Marcus Schenkenberg
and Stephanie Seymour
Fall/Winter 1993/94

65. Kristen McMenamy
and Nadja Auermann
*Spring/Summer 1995,
Atelier*

66. Marcus Schenkenberg
and Stephanie Seymour
Fall/Winter 1993/94

67. Jason Savas and Pina
Fall/Winter 1981/82

68. Stephanie Seymour and
Marcus Schenkenberg
Fall/Winter 1993/94

69. Kristen McMenamy
*Spring/Summer 1995,
Atelier*

70. Claudia Schiffer and Stan Nelson
Fall/Winter 1994/95

72. Kristen McMenamy
and Nadja Auermann
*Spring/Summer 1995,
Atelier*

73. Kristen McMenamy and
Nadja Auermann
*Spring/Summer 1995,
Atelier*

74. Lina. Marcus Abel
and Antonia
Fall/Winter 1981/82

75. Stephanie Seymour and
Marcus Schenkenberg
Fall/Winter 1993/94

76. Stephanie Seymour and
Marcus Schenkenberg
Fall/Winter 1993/94

77. Elton John
Spring/Summer 1997

Gath- ering Moss

81. Kate Moss
Fall/Winter 1996/97

82. Elton John
Spring/Summer 1997

83. Kate Moss
Fall/Winter 1996/97

84. Kate Moss
Fall/Winter 1996/97

85. The Artist Formerly
Known as Prince
Fall/Winter 1995/96

86. Kate Moss
Fall/Winter 1996/97

87. Jon Bon Jovi
Spring/Summer 1997

88. Kate Moss
Fall/Winter 1996/97

93. Kate Moss
Fall/Winter 1996/97

89.-92. Kate Moss
Fall/Winter 1996/97

94. Kate Moss
Fall/Winter 1996/97

95. Kristen McMenamy
Fall/Winter 1997/98

96. Courtney Love
Spring/Summer 1998

97. Kate Moss
Fall/Winter 1996/97

  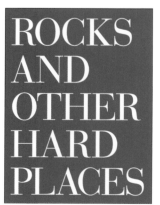 

98. Stella Tennant
*Fall/Winter 1997/98,
Atelier*

99. Kate Moss
Fall/Winter 1996/97

ROCKS
AND
OTHER
HARD
PLACES

103. Janice Dickinson
Spring/Summer 1983

104. Linda Evangelista,
Christy Turlington and Brynja
Spring/Summer 1988

106. Linda Evangelista
Spring/Summer 1988

108. Scott Benoit, Christy Turlington,
Linda Evangelista, John Enos and Brynja
Spring/Summer 1988

110. Bill Skinner, Linda Spierings, Paul Vasbotten,
Claudia Mason, Meg Grosswendt and Scott Benoit
Fall/Winter 1986/87

112. Christy Turlington, Hoyt Richards and John Enos
Spring/Summer 1987

114. Lauren Helm, Janice Dickinson and Iman
Spring/Summer 1983

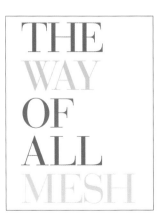

117. Kara Young and
Reinaldo
*Spring/Summer 1995,
Home*

THE
WAY
OF
ALL
MESH

121. Stella Tennant
*Fall/Winter 1997/98,
Atelier*

122. Stan Nelson, Nadja Auermann, Marcus
Schenkenberg, Cindy Crawford, Stephanie
Seymour, Vladimir, Claudia Schiffer, Rick
Arango, Christy Turlington and Maximo
Fall/Winter 1994/95

124. Elton John
Spring/Summer 1997

125. Cindy Crawford
Fall/Winter 1994/95

126. Nadja Auermann, Christy Turlington,
Claudia Schiffer, Cindy Crawford and
Stephanie Seymour
Fall/Winter 1994/95

128. Stan Nelson and
Claudia Schiffer
Fall/Winter 1994/95

129. Vladimir
Fall/Winter 1994/95

130. Patricia Arquette
*Fall/Winter 1997/98,
Atelier*

131. Stella Tennant
*Fall/Winter 1997/98,
Atelier*

132. Stephanie Seymour
Fall/Winter 1993/94

134. Marcus Schenkenberg
Fall/Winter 1993/94

135. Elton John
Spring/Summer 1997

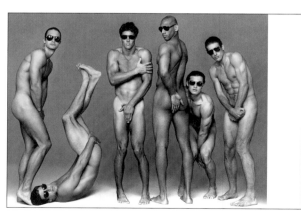

136. Marcus Schenkenberg, Eric Etebari, Rick
Arango, Vladimir, Stan Nelson and Maximo
Fall/Winter 1994/95, Accessories

Look Home-ward, Angel

141. Joel West and
Alex Lundqvist
Spring/Summer 1997,
Home

142. Johny Zander. Jason Lewis. Naomi Campbell.
Kristen McMenamy. Sascha. Christina Kruse and
Trish Goff   *Spring/Summer 1996, Home*
143. Sylvester Stallone and Claudia Schiffer
Spring/Summer 1995, Home

144. Nadja Auermann and Claudia Schiffer
Spring/Summer 1995, Home

146. Amy Wesson. Kylie Bax. Kirsten Owen.
Joel West. Bruno Saladini. Stella Tennant
and Alex Lundqvist
Spring/Summer 1997, Home

148. Jon Bon Jovi
Spring/Summer 1997,
Home

149. Trish Goff
Spring/Summer 1997,
Home

150. Beverly Johnson. Danny Arguelles. Lisa Taylor.
Kim Alexis. Marcus Abel. Rosie Vela.
Brian Tinkham. Kelly LeBrock. Jeff Aquilon
and Jason Savas
Spring/Summer 1981

152. Naomi Campbell
Spring/Summer 1996,
Home

154. Alex Lundqvist. Stella Tennant. Tasha Tilberg.
Christian Anderson. Kylie Bax. Kirsten Owen.
Joel West. Bruno Saladini and Amy Wesson
Spring/Summer 1997, Home
155. Christian Anderson *Spring/Summer 1997, Home*

156. Alex Lundqvist
Spring/Summer 1997,
Home

157. Kylie Bax and
Stella Tennant
Spring/Summer 1997,
Home

158. Naomi Campbell and
Kristen McMenamy
Spring/Summer 1996,
Home

159. Charles Andrews
Spring/Summer 1996,
Home

160. Marcus Schenkenberg
Fall/Winter 1993/94, Home

162. Christy Turlington, Nadja Auermann,
Cindy Crawford, Stephanie Seymour and
Claudia Schiffer
Fall/Winter 1994/95

164. Claudia Schiffer
Fall/Winter 1994/95,
Home

165. Nadja Auermann
Fall/Winter 1995/96,
Home

166. Alex Lundqvist and Kylie Bax
Spring/Summer 1997, Home

A Quick Stitch In Time

170. Sebastian Kim
Spring/Summer 1998,
Atelier

171. Erin O'Connor
Spring/Summer 1998,
Atelier

172. Donatella Versace
Blonde

Endpapers
Kate Moss
Fall/Winter 1996/97

Tempis Fugit

Spring/Summer 1980

Marcus Abel, Alessandro, Pat Anderson, Matt Collins, Janice Dickinson, Gia, Jerry Hall, Tony Hamilton, Patti Hansen, Ken Robert, Rene Russo, Jason Savas, Eric Scott, Tony Spinelli and Rosie Vela
Maury Hopson, *hair*
Sophie Levy, *makeup*
Paul Cavaco, *stylist*

Fall/Winter 1980/81

Kim Alexis, Janice Dickinson, Gia, Margaux Hemingway, Brooke Shields, Tony Spinelli, Lisa Vale and Scott Webster
Suga, *hair*
Way Bandy, *makeup*
Donatella Versace and Paul Beck, *stylists*

Spring/Summer 1981

Marcus Abel, Kim Alexis, Jeff Aquilon, Danny Arguelles, Adam Dixon, Beverly Johnson, Kelly LeBrock, Jason Savas, Lisa Taylor, Brian Tinkham and Rosie Vela
Suga, *hair*
Ariella, *makeup*
Paul Cavaco, *stylist*

Fall/Winter 1981/82

Marcus Abel, Alessandro, Kim Alexis, Antonia, Dante, Iman, Kelly LeBrock, Leo, Peter Lepore, Lina, Luisa, Pina, Anne Rohart, Rene Russo, Jason Savas, Edourdo Stoppi, Paolo Stoppi, Rosie Vela and Ed Zimlinghaus
Suga, *hair*
Way Bandy, *makeup*
Donatella Versace and Paul Beck, *stylists*

Spring/Summer 1982

Jackie Adams, Joe Dakota, Rick Edwards, Quentin Hunt, Rosemary McGrotha, Kathryn Redding, Jason Savas, Annette Stai and Rosie Vela
Suga, *hair*
Nando Chiese, *makeup*
Paul Cavaco, *stylist*

Fall/Winter 1982/83

Jackie Adams, Grant Alexander, Kim Alexis, Danny Arguelles, Joe Dakota, Rick Edwards, Kelly Emberg, Eric, Gia, Jerry Hall, Tony Hamilton, Quentin Hunt, Beverly Johnson, Ken King, Mitch Oprea and Rosie Vela
Suga, *hair*
Ariella and Leonardo de Vega, *makeup*
Donatella Versace and Paul Beck, *stylists*
Robert Currie and Larry Arfield, *set design*

Spring/Summer 1983

Danny Arguelles, Attila, Jeff Aquilon, Janice Dickinson, Jerry Hall, Tony Hamilton, Lauren Helm, Quentin Hunt, Iman and Lynne Koester
Suga, *hair*
Ariella, *makeup*
Donatella Versace and Paul Beck, *stylists*
Robert Currie and Larry Arfield, *set design*

Fall/Winter 1983/84

Janice Dickinson, Beverly Johnson, Renee Simonsen and Rosie Vela
Suga, *hair*
Ariella, *makeup*
Donatella Versace and Paul Beck, *stylists*

Spring/Summer 1984

Kim Alexis, Bonnie Berman, Kelly LeBrock, Tim Clements, Janice Dickinson, Tom Hill, Iman, Andie MacDowell and Bill Shelley
Suga, *hair*
Ariella, *makeup*
Donatella Versace and Paul Beck, *stylists*

Fall/Winter 1984

Josie Borain, Danny, Janice Dickinson, Leticia Lucas, Talisa Soto and Jen Yarrow
Suga, *hair*
Ariella, *makeup*
Donatella Versace and Paul Beck, *stylists*

Fall/Winter 1986/87
Scott Benoit, Meg Grosswendt, Claudia Mason,
Bill Skinner, Linda Spierings and Paul Vasbotten
Suga, *hair*
Ariella, *makeup*
Donatella Versace and Paul Beck, *stylists*
Robert Currie and Larry Arfield, *set design*

Spring/Summer 1987
Cindy Crawford, John Enos, Estelle Lefebure, Lenita,
Paulina Porizkova, Hoyt Richards, Christy Turlington
and Eric Walters
Suga, *hair*
Ariella and Kevyn Aucoin, *makeup*
Donatella Versace and Paul Beck, *stylists*

Spring/Summer 1988
Scott Benoit, Brynja, Curt, John Enos, Linda
Evangelista, Paulina Porizkova, Christy Turlington and
Eric Walters
Suga, *hair*
Ariella, *makeup*
Donatella Versace and Paul Beck, *stylists*
Robert Currie and Larry Arfield, *set design*

Spring/Summer 1993
Aya, Naomi Campbell, Linda Evangelista, Kristen
McMenamy, Kate Moss, Nick Moss, Stephanie
Seymour, Shalom Harlow, Christy Turlington and Yvette
Oribe, *hair*
François Nars, *makeup*
Simone Colina, *stylist*
Robert Currie and Larry Arfield, *set design*

Fall/Winter 1993/94
Marcus Schenkenberg and Stephanie Seymour
Oribe, *hair*
François Nars, *makeup*
Simone Colina, *stylist*

Spring/Summer 1994
Daniel de la Falaise, Linda Evangelista and
Stan Nelson
Oribe, *hair*
François Nars, *makeup*
Nicoletta Santoro, *stylist*

Fall/Winter 1994/95
Rick Arango, Nadja Auermann, Chance, Cindy
Crawford, Eric Etebari, Maximo, Stan Nelson,
Marcus Schenkenberg, Claudia Schiffer, Stephanie
Seymour, Christy Turlington and Vladimir
Yannick d'Is, *hair*
François Nars, *makeup*
Simone Colina, *stylist*

Spring/Summer 1995, Atelier/Home
Nadja Auermann, Elton John, Kristen McMenamy,
Reinaldo, Claudia Schiffer, Sylvester Stallone
and Kara Young
Oribe, *hair*
François Nars, *makeup*
Carlyne Cerf de Dudzeele, *stylist*
Marla Weinhoff, *set design*

"Blonde" Campaign, 1995
Donatella Versace
Oribe, *hair*
François Nars, *makeup*

Fall/Winter 1995/96
The Artist Formerly Known as Prince, Mike Campbell,
Trish Goff, Kristen McMenamy, Shalom Harlow and
Amber Valletta
Oribe, *hair*
François Nars, *makeup*
Donatella Versace, *stylist*

Spring/Summer 1996, Home
Charles Andrews, Elizabeth Hurley and
Amber Valletta
Guido Palau, *hair*
François Nars, *makeup*
Joe McKenna, *stylist*

Spring/Summer 1996, Home
Naomi Campbell, Trish Goff, Christina Kruse, Jason
Lewis, Kristen McMenamy, Sascha, Amber Valletta
and Johnny Zander
Guido Palau, *hair*
François Nars, *makeup*
Joe McKenna, *stylist*
Marla Weinhoff, *set design*

Spring/Summer 1996, Atelier
Stella Tennant
Guido Palau, *hair*
François Nars, *makeup*
Joe McKenna, *stylist*

Fall/Winter 1996/97
Kate Moss
Guido Palau, *hair*
François Nars, *makeup*
Joe McKenna, *stylist*

Spring/Summer 1997
Elton John
Ron Fretz, *hair*
Linda Cantello, *makeup*
Nicoletta Santoro, *stylist*

Spring/Summer 1997
Donatella Versace
Guido Palau, *hair*
François Nars, *makeup*

Spring/Summer 1997
Kylie Bax, Jon Bon Jovi, Stella Tennant,
Tasha Tilberg and Amy Wesson
Carlos Merlo, *hair*
François Nars, *makeup*
Joe McKenna, *stylist*

Spring/Summer 1997, Home
Christian Anderson, Kylie Bax, Trish Goff,
Alex Lundqvist, Kirsten Owen, Bruno Saladini, Stella
Tennant, Tasha Tilberg, Amy Wesson and Joel West
Guido Palau, *hair*
François Nars, *makeup*
Nicoletta Santoro, *stylist*
Marla Weinhoff, *set design*

Fall/Winter 1997/98
Edward Fogg, Kristen McMenamy, Kees Poort and
Michael Walton
Guido Palau, *hair*
François Nars and Ayako, *makeup*
Joe McKenna, *stylist*

Fall/Winter 1997/98
Scott Barnhill, Karen Elson, Edward Fogg, Georgina
Grenville, Jolijn, Ramsay Jones, Christina Kruse,
Jason Lewis, Alex Lundqvist, Keith Mallos, Kristen
McMenamy, Franco Musso, Chandra North, Kirsten
Owen, Jamie Rishar, Thorsten and Mark Vanderloo
Guido Palau, *hair*
François Nars, *makeup*
Joe McKenna, *stylist*

Fall/Winter 1997/98, Atelier
Patricia Arquette and Stella Tennant
Guido Palau, *hair*
François Nars, *makeup*
Nicoletta Santoro, *stylist*

Spring/Summer 1998
Courtney Love and Erin O'Connor
Guido Palau, *hair*
Linda Cantello, *makeup*
Joe McKenna, *stylist*

Spring/Summer 1998, Atelier
Sebastian Kim and Erin O'Connor
Guido Palau, *hair*
James Kaliardos, *makeup*
Nicoletta Santoro, *stylist*

Grazie...Prego

RUTH ANSEL
DOON ARBUS
ANGELO AZZENA
BILL BACHMANN
BOB BISHOP
BRUNO BUGIANI
PAUL CHAN
PATRIZIA CUCCO
SHARON DELANO
JOHN EDELMANN
BONNIE FALKENBERG
ELISA FERRI
VERLIE FISHER
MARGARET FODALE
MARGOT FRANKEL
KARA GLYNN
SADIE HALL
BRIAN HETHERINGTON
RUEDI HOFMANN
MARK HOLBORN
SEBASTIAN KIM
GIDEON LEWIN
LING LI
DAVID LIITTSCHWAGER
JIM MACARI
PAOLA MARLETTA
MARC MCCLISH
LARS NORD
SCOTT NORKIN
MARELLA PETTINI
JEFFREY POSTERNAK
MARC ROYCE
SARA RUDNER
NORMA STEVENS
JIM VARRIALE
ANDREW WYLIE

Published by Jonathan Cape 1998

1 3 5 7 9 10 8 6 4 2

© Gianni Versace S.p.A and Richard Avedon 1998

First published in Great Britain in 1998 by
Jonathan Cape
Random House, 20 Vauxhall Bridge Road, London SW1V 2SA

Random House Australia (Pty) Limited
20 Alfred Street, Milsons Point, Sydney,
New South Wales 2061, Australia

Random House New Zealand Limited
18 Poland Road, Glenfield,
Auckland 10, New Zealand

Random House South Africa (Pty) Limited
Endulini, 5A Jubilee Road, Parktown 2193, South Africa

Random House UK Limited Reg. No. 954009

A CIP catalogue record for this book is available from the British Library

ISBN 0-224-04193-2

Printed in Italy by Amilcare Pizzi S.p.A, Milan

DESIGNED BY MARY SHANAHAN